Hats &

Staying warm and looking stylish can be one and the same!
These scarves, hats, and cowls to crochet are fashionable accents,
perfect for any wardrobe. The scarves offer beautiful shapes and
textures, while the hats include must-have slouch designs, a chic
brimmed cap, and a trendy chullo. When the chill wind of winter is
blowing, the cowls are delightfully cozy. They're all fabulous gifts for
family and friends—just don't forget to crochet a few for yourself!

LEISURE ARTS, INC.
Little Rock, Arkansas

QUICK SCARF

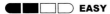 **EASY**

Finished Size: 3½" wide x 65" long (9 cm x 165 cm)

SHOPPING LIST

Yarn
(Super Bulky Weight) **SUPER BULKY 6**
[6 ounces, 106 yards
(170 grams, 97 meters) per skein]:
☐ One skein

Crochet Hook
☐ Size P/Q (15 mm)
or size needed for gauge

GAUGE INFORMATION
Gauge Swatch: 3½" wide x 5" high
(9 cm x 12.75 cm)
Work same as Scarf for 2 rows; do
not finish off.

INSTRUCTIONS
Row 1: Ch 4, (4 dc, ch 3, slip st) in
fourth ch from hook.

Row 2: Ch 3, turn; (4 dc, ch 3, slip st)
in first ch-3 sp.

Repeat Row 2 for pattern until
Scarf measures approximately
65" (165 cm) from beginning
or until desired length.

Finish off.

SOFT RUFFLY SCARF

 **EASY**

Finished Size: 4" wide x 72" long (10 cm x 183 cm)

SHOPPING LIST

Yarn (Bulky Weight)
[6 ounces, 185 yards
(170 grams, 169 meters)
per skein]:
☐ One skein

Crochet Hook
☐ Size M/N (9 mm)
or size needed for gauge

GAUGE INFORMATION

In pattern, 7 dc = 4" (10 cm)
Gauge Swatch: 4" wide x 4½" high
(10 cm x 11.5 cm)
Ch 9.
Row 1: Dc in fourth ch from hook
(3 skipped chs count as first dc)
and in each ch across: 7 dc.
Rows 2-6: Ch 3 **(counts as first dc)**,
turn; dc in next dc and in each dc
across.
Finish off.

INSTRUCTIONS
Ch 122.

Rnd 1 (Right side)**:** 4 Dc in fourth ch
from hook **(3 skipped chs count as
first dc)**, dc in next ch and in each
ch across to last ch, 9 dc in last ch;
working in free loops of beginning
ch *(Fig. 3b, page 44)*, dc in next ch
and in each ch across; 4 dc in same
ch as first dc; join with slip st to first
dc: 252 dc.

Rnd 2: Ch 4 **(counts as first dc plus
ch 1)**, dc in same st, ch 1, (dc, ch 1)
twice in next dc and in each dc
around; join with slip st to first dc,
finish off.

MULTICOLORED SET

 **INTERMEDIATE**

SHOPPING LIST

Yarn (Medium Weight)
[3.5 ounces, 170 yards
(100 grams, 156 meters) per skein]:

Hat
☐ Blue - One skein
☐ Lt Green - One skein
☐ Green - One skein

Scarf
☐ Blue - 3 skeins
☐ Lt Green - 2 skeins
☐ Green - 2 skeins

Crochet Hook
☐ Size I (5.5 mm)
or size needed for gauge

Additional Supplies
☐ Yarn needle

SIZE INFORMATION

Hat: Fits head circumference
20-22" (51-56 cm)
Scarf: 9" wide x 80½" long
(23 cm x 204.5 cm)

GAUGE INFORMATION

In pattern,
one repeat (8 hdc) = 2½"
(6.25 cm);
Rows 1-5 = 2¾" (7 cm)
Gauge Swatch:
5¼" wide x 3½" high
(13.25 cm x 9 cm)
With Lt Green, ch 18.
Work same as Scarf for 6 rows.
Finish off.

STITCH GUIDE

TREBLE CROCHET *(abbreviated tr)*
YO twice, insert hook in st indicated, YO and pull up a loop (4 loops on hook), (YO and draw through 2 loops on hook) 3 times.

DOUBLE TREBLE CROCHET
(abbreviated dtr)
YO 3 times, insert hook in st indicated, YO and pull up a loop (5 loops on hook), (YO and draw through 2 loops on hook) 4 times.

**HALF DOUBLE
CROCHET 2 TOGETHER**
(abbreviated hdc2tog)
(uses next 2 sts)
(YO, insert hook in **next** st, YO and pull up a loop) twice, YO and draw through all 5 loops on hook (**counts as one hdc**).

DOUBLE CROCHET 2 TOGETHER
(abbreviated dc2tog)
(uses next 3 sts)
★ YO, insert hook in **next** st, YO and pull up a loop, YO and draw through 2 loops on hook; repeat from ★ 2 times **more**, YO and draw through all 4 loops on hook (**counts as one dc**).

**DOUBLE TREBLE
CROCHET 2 TOGETHER**
(abbreviated dtr2tog)
(uses next 3 dc)
★ YO 3 times, insert hook in **next** dc YO and pull up a loop, (YO and draw through 2 loops on hook) 3 times; repeat from ★ 2 times **more**, YO and draw through all 4 loops on hook (**counts as one dtr**).

INSTRUCTIONS
Hat
BODY
With Blue, ch 64; being careful **not** to twist ch, join with slip st to form a ring.

Rnd 1 (Right side)**:** Ch 5 (**counts as first dtr, now and throughout**), dtr in same st, ★ † tr in next ch, dc in next ch, hdc in next ch, sc in next ch, hdc in next ch, dc in next ch, tr in next ch †, 3 dtr in next ch; repeat from ★ around to last 7 chs, then repeat from † to † once, dtr in same st as first dtr; join with slip st to first dtr changing to Green *(Fig. 4b, page 45)*; cut Blue: 80 sts.

Rnd 2: Ch 3 (**counts as first dc**), dc in same st and in next 3 sts, dc2tog, dc in next 3 sts, ★ 3 dc in next dtr, dc in next 3 sts, dc2tog, dc in next 3 sts; repeat from ★ around, dc in same st as first dc; join with slip st to first dc changing to Blue; cut Green.

Rnd 3: Ch 1, sc in same st, ★ † hdc in next dc, dc in next dc, tr in next dc, dtr2tog, tr in next dc, dc in next dc, hdc in next dc †, sc in next dc; repeat from ★ around to last 9 dc, then repeat from † to † once; join with slip st to first sc changing to Lt Green; cut Blue: 64 sts.

Rnd 4: Ch 2 (**counts as first hdc, now and throughout**), hdc in next st and in each st around; join with slip st to first hdc.

Rnd 5: Ch 2, hdc in next hdc and in each hdc around; join with slip st to first hdc changing to Blue; cut Lt Green.

Rnd 6: Ch 5, dtr in same st, ★ † tr in next hdc, dc in next hdc, hdc in next hdc, sc in next hdc, hdc in next hdc, dc in next hdc, tr in next hdc †, 3 dtr in next hdc; repeat from ★ around to last 7 hdc, then repeat from † to † once, dtr in same st as first dtr; join with slip st to first dtr changing to Green; cut Blue: 80 sts.

Rnds 7-13: Repeat Rnds 2-6 once, then repeat Rnds 2 and 3 once **more**: 64 sts.

CROWN

Rnd 1: Ch 2, hdc in next 5 sts, hdc2tog, (hdc in next 6 sts, hdc2tog) around; join with slip st to first hdc: 56 sts.

Rnd 2: Ch 2, hdc in next 4 hdc, hdc2tog, (hdc in next 5 hdc, hdc2tog) around; join with slip st to first hdc changing to Blue; cut Lt Green: 48 sts.

Rnd 3: Ch 2, hdc2tog, (hdc in next hdc, hdc2tog) around; join with slip st to first hdc: 32 sts.

Rnd 4: Ch 2, hdc in next hdc, hdc2tog, (hdc in next 2 hdc, hdc2tog) around; join with slip st to first hdc changing to Lt Green; cut Blue: 24 sts.

Rnd 5: Ch 2, hdc in next hdc, hdc2tog, (hdc in next 2 hdc, hdc2tog) around; join with slip st to first hdc: 18 sts.

Rnd 6: Ch 1, YO, insert hook in same st, YO and pull up a loop, YO, insert hook in next hdc, YO and pull up a loop, YO and draw through all 5 loops on hook (**counts as one hdc**), hdc2tog around; join with slip st to first hdc, finish off leaving a long end for sewing: 9 sts.

Thread yarn needle with long end and weave through remaining 9 hdc on Rnd 6; gather **tightly** to close and secure end.

TRIM

Rnd 1: With **right** side facing and working in free loops of beginning ch *(Fig. 3b, page 44)*, join Lt Green with sc in first ch *(see Joining With Sc, page 44)*; sc in next ch and in each ch around; join with slip st to first sc: 64 sc.

Rnd 2: Working from **left** to **right**, work reverse sc in each sc around *(Figs. 6a-d, page 46)*; join with slip st to first st, finish off.

Scarf

With Lt Green, ch 258.

Row 1 (Right side)**:** Hdc in back ridge of third ch from hook and each ch across (**2 skipped chs count as first hdc**): 257 hdc.

Row 2: Ch 2, turn; hdc in next hdc and in each hdc across changing to Blue in last hdc made *(Fig. 4a, page 45)*; cut Lt Green.

Row 3: Ch 5, turn; dtr in first hdc, ★ † tr in next hdc, dc in next hdc, hdc in next hdc, sc in next hdc, hdc in next hdc, dc in next hdc, tr in next hdc †, 3 dtr in next hdc; repeat from ★ across to last 8 hdc, then repeat from † to † once, 2 dtr in last hdc changing to Green in last dtr made; cut Blue: 321 sts.

Row 4: Ch 3 **(counts as first dc)**, turn; dc in first dtr, ★ † dc in next 3 sts, dc2tog, dc in next 3 sts †, 3 dc in next st; repeat from ★ across to last 10 sts, then repeat from † to † once, 2 dc in last dtr changing to Blue in last dc made; cut Green.

Row 5: Ch 1, turn; sc in first dc, ★ hdc in next dc, dc in next dc, tr in next dc, dtr2tog, tr in next dc, dc in next dc, hdc in next dc, sc in next dc; repeat from ★ across, changing to Lt Green in last sc made; cut Blue: 257 sts.

Row 6: Ch 2, turn; hdc in next hdc and in each st across.

Rows 7-16: Repeat Rows 2-6 twice.

Row 17: Ch 2, turn; hdc in next hdc and in each hdc across; finish off.

CABLED SLOUCHY SET

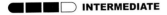 **INTERMEDIATE**

SHOPPING LIST

Yarn (Medium Weight)
[3.5 ounces, 177 yards
(100 grams, 162 meters) per skein]:
- ☐ **Hat** - 2 skeins
- ☐ **Scarf** - 3 skeins

Crochet Hook
- ☐ Size I (5.5 mm)
  or size needed for gauge

Additional Supplies
- ☐ Yarn needle

SIZE INFORMATION

Hat: Fits head circumference 20-22"
  (51-56 cm)
Scarf: 6½" wide x 38" long
  (16.5 cm x 96.5 cm)

GAUGE INFORMATION

In pattern,
  2 repeats (16 sts) = 4¾" (12 cm);
  11 rows = 3½" (9 cm)
Gauge Swatch: 3½" (9 cm) square
Ch 13.
Row 1: Hdc in third ch from hook
and in each ch across (**2 skipped
chs count as first hdc**): 12 hdc.
Rows 2-11: Ch 2 (**counts as first
hdc**), turn; hdc in next hdc and in
each hdc across.
Finish off.

——— STITCH GUIDE ———

FRONT POST TREBLE CROCHET
   (abbreviated FPtr)

YO twice, insert hook from **front** to **back** around post of st indicated *(Fig. 5, page 45)*, YO and pull up a loop (4 loops on hook), (YO and draw through 2 loops on hook) 3 times. Skip st behind FPtr.

FRONT POST DOUBLE TREBLE CROCHET *(abbreviated FPdtr)*

YO 3 times, insert hook from **front** to **back** around post of st indicated *(Fig. 5, page 45)*, YO and pull up a loop (5 loops on hook), (YO and draw through 2 loops on hook) 4 times. Skip st behind FPdtr.

HALF DOUBLE CROCHET 2 TOGETHER *(abbreviated hdc2tog)*
   (uses next 2 sts)

(YO, insert hook in **next** st, YO and pull up a loop) twice, YO and draw through all 5 loops on hook (**counts as one hdc**).

INSTRUCTIONS
Hat
RIBBING

Ch 7.

Row 1: Sc in back ridge of second ch from hook and each ch across *(Fig. 1, page 44)*: 6 sc.

Row 2: Ch 1, turn; sc in Back Loop Only of each sc across *(Fig. 2, page 44)*.

Repeat Row 2 until Ribbing measures approximately 19" (48.5 cm) from beginning ch when slightly stretched.

Joining Row (Wrong side)**:** Ch 1, turn; matching free loops of beginning ch *(Fig. A)* to sc on last row, slip st in each st across working in Back Loops Only of **both** layers; do **not** finish off.

Turn Ribbing **right** side out.

Fig. A

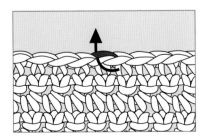

BODY

Rnd 1 (Right side)**:** With **right** side facing, ch 2 (**counts as first hdc, now and throughout**), work 63 hdc evenly spaced around in ends of rows; join with slip st to first hdc: 64 hdc.

Rnd 2: Ch 2, hdc in next hdc and in each st around; join with slip st to first hdc.

Rnd 3: Ch 2, hdc in next 3 hdc, work FPtr around st one rnd **below** each of next 4 sts, ★ hdc in next 4 hdc, work FPtr around st one rnd **below** each of next 4 sts; repeat from ★ around; join with slip st to first hdc.

Rnd 4: Ch 2, hdc in next hdc and in each st around; join with slip st to first hdc.

Rnd 5: Ch 2, hdc in next 3 hdc, skip next 2 FPtr one rnd **below**, work FPdtr around each of next 2 FPtr, working in **front** of last 2 FPdtr just made, work FPdtr around each of 2 skipped FPtr, ★ hdc in next 4 hdc, skip next 2 FPtr one rnd **below**, work FPdtr around each of next 2 FPtr, working in **front** of last 2 FPdtr just made, work FPdtr around each of 2 skipped FPtr; repeat from ★ around; join with slip st to first hdc.

Repeat Rnds 2-5 until piece measures approximately 8" (20.5 cm) from bottom edge, ending by working Rnd 5; do **not** finish off.

CROWN

Rnd 1: Ch 2, hdc2tog, (hdc in next 6 sts, hdc2tog) around to last 5 sts, hdc in last 5 sts; join with slip st to first hdc: 56 hdc.

Rnd 2: Ch 2, hdc2tog, work FPtr around each of next 4 FPdtr one rnd **below**, ★ hdc2tog, hdc in next hdc, work FPtr around each of next 4 FPdtr one rnd **below**; repeat from ★ around; join with slip st to first hdc: 48 sts.

Rnd 3: Ch 2, hdc2tog, (hdc in next 2 sts, hdc2tog) around to last FPtr, hdc in last FPtr; join with slip st to first hdc: 36 hdc.

Rnd 4: Ch 2, hdc2tog, (hdc in next hdc, hdc2tog) around; join with slip st to first hdc: 24 hdc.

Rnds 5 and 6: Ch 1, YO, insert hook in same st, YO and pull up a loop, YO, insert hook in next hdc, YO and pull up a loop, YO and draw through all 5 loops on hook (**counts as one hdc**), hdc2tog around; join with slip st to first hdc: 6 sts.

Finish off, leaving a long end for sewing.

Thread yarn needle with long end and weave needle through remaining hdc on Rnd 6; gather **tightly** to close and secure end.

Scarf
Ch 129.

Row 1 (Right side)**:** Hdc in back ridge of third ch from hook and each ch across (**2 skipped chs count as first hdc**): 128 hdc.

Row 2: Ch 2, turn; hdc in next hdc and in each st across.

Row 3: Ch 2, turn; hdc in next hdc, work FPtr around st one row **below** each of next 4 sts, ★ hdc in next 4 sts, work FPtr around st one row **below** each of next 4 sts; repeat from ★ across to last 2 hdc, hdc in last 2 hdc.

Row 4: Ch 2, turn; hdc in next hdc and in each st across.

Row 5: Ch 2, turn; hdc in next hdc, skip next 2 FPtr one row **below**, work FPdtr around each of next 2 FPtr, working in **front** of last 2 FPdtr just made, work FPdtr around each of 2 skipped FPtr, ★ hdc in next 4 hdc, skip next 2 FPtr one row **below**, work FPdtr around each of next 2 FPtr, working in **front** of last 2 FPdtr just made, work FPdtr around each of 2 skipped FPtr; repeat from ★ across to last 2 hdc, hdc in last 2 hdc.

Rows 6-8: Repeat Rows 2-4.

Row 9: Ch 2, turn; hdc in next hdc, skip next 2 FPtr one row **below**, work FPdtr around each of next 2 FPtr, working in **front** of last 2 FPdtr just made, work FPdtr around each of 2 skipped FPtr, † hdc in next 4 hdc, skip next 2 FPtr one row **below**, work FPdtr around each of next 2 FPtr, working in **front** of last 2 FPdtr just made, work FPdtr around each of 2 skipped FPtr †; repeat from † to † 2 times **more**, ch 4 (opening), skip next 4 hdc and next 2 FPtr one row **below**, work FPdtr around each of next 2 FPtr, working in **front** of last 2 FPdtr just made, work FPdtr around each of 2 skipped FPtr, repeat from † to † across to last 2 hdc, hdc in last 2 hdc: 124 sts and one ch-4 sp.

Row 10: Ch 2, turn; hdc in next hdc and in each st across to next ch-4 sp, † hdc in next ch-4 sp, hdc in next st and in each st across: 128 hdc.

Rows 11-13: Repeat Rows 3-5.

Rows 14-20: Repeat Rows 2-5 once, then repeat Rows 2-4 once **more**.

Finish off.

REVERSIBLE SCARF

 **EASY**

Finished Size: 7½" wide x 80" long (19 cm x 203 cm)

SHOPPING LIST

Yarn (Medium Weight)
[3.5 ounces, 170 yards
(100 grams, 156 meters)
per skein]:
- ☐ Blue - 2 skeins
- ☐ Taupe - 2 skeins

Crochet Hook
- ☐ Size I (5.5 mm)
  or size needed for gauge

GAUGE INFORMATION
Gauge Swatch: 7½" wide x 4" high
(19 cm x 10 cm)
Work same as Scarf for 12 rows; do
not finish off.

——— STITCH GUIDE ———
LONG DOUBLE CROCHET
(abbreviated Ldc)
YO, insert hook in sc in row **below**
next hdc, YO and pull up a loop
even with last st made, (YO and
draw through 2 loops on hook)
twice *(Fig. A)*.

Fig. A

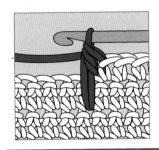

INSTRUCTIONS
With Blue, ch 24.

Row 1: Sc in second ch from hook
and in each ch across: 23 sts.

When changing colors *(Fig. 4a, page 45)*, do **not** cut yarn, carry unused yarn **loosely** along edge.

Row 2: Ch 2 (**counts as first hdc, now and throughout**), turn; hdc in next sc and in each sc across, changing to Taupe in last hdc made.

Row 3: Ch 1, turn; sc in first 3 hdc, (work Ldc, sc in next 3 hdc) across.

Row 4: Ch 2, turn; hdc in next sc and in each st across, changing to Blue in last hdc made.

Row 5: Ch 1, turn; sc in first hdc, work Ldc, (sc in next 3 hdc, work Ldc) across to last hdc, sc in last hdc.

Row 6: Ch 2, turn; hdc in next st and in each st across, changing to Taupe in last hdc made.

Repeat Rows 3-6 for pattern until Scarf measures approximately 80" (203 cm) from beginning ch, ending by working Row 6; at end of last row, do **not** change colors; cut Taupe and finish off Blue.

BRIMMED CAP

Shown on page 23.

 **EASY**

Finished Size: Fits head circumference 20-22" (51-56 cm)

SHOPPING LIST

Yarn (Medium Weight)
[3 ounces, 145 yards
(85 grams, 133 meters) per skein]:
☐ 2 skeins

Crochet Hooks
☐ Size K (6.5 mm) **and**
☐ Size L (8 mm)
or sizes needed for gauge

Additional Supplies
☐ Straight pins
☐ Yarn needle
☐ Sewing needle
☐ Matching thread
☐ 1¼" (32 mm) Buttons - 2

Cap is worked holding two strands
of yarn together throughout.

GAUGE INFORMATION
Gauge Swatch:
4" (10 cm) diameter
Work same as Body for 4 rnds; do
not finish off.

── STITCH GUIDE ──
**BEGINNING SINGLE
CROCHET 2 TOGETHER**
(abbreviated beginning sc2tog)
Pull up a loop in each of first 2 sc,
YO and draw through all 3 loops on
hook (**counts as one sc**).
SINGLE CROCHET 2 TOGETHER
(abbreviated sc2tog)
Pull up a loop in each of next 2 sc,
YO and draw through all 3 loops on
hook (**counts as one sc**).

INSTRUCTIONS
BODY
With larger size hook, ch 4; join with
slip st to form a ring.

Rnd 1 (Right side)**:** Ch 1, 7 sc in ring;
join with slip st to first sc.

Note: Loop a short piece of yarn
around any stitch to mark Rnd 1 as
right side.

Rnd 2: Ch 1, 2 sc in same st and in each sc around; join with slip st to first sc: 14 sc.

Rnd 3: Ch 1, sc in same st, 2 sc in next sc, (sc in next sc, 2 sc in next sc) around; join with slip st to first sc: 21 sc.

Rnd 4: Ch 1, sc in same st and in next sc, 2 sc in next sc, (sc in next 2 sc, 2 sc in next sc) around; join with slip st to first sc: 28 sc.

Rnd 5: Ch 1, sc in same st and in next 2 sc, 2 sc in next sc, (sc in next 3 sc, 2 sc in next sc) around; join with slip st to first sc: 35 sc.

Rnd 6: Ch 1, sc in same st and in next 3 sc, 2 sc in next sc, (sc in next 4 sc, 2 sc in next sc) around; join with slip st to first sc: 42 sc.

Rnd 7: Ch 1, sc in same st and in next 4 sc, 2 sc in next sc, (sc in next 5 sc, 2 sc in next sc) around; join with slip st to first sc: 49 sc.

Rnd 8: Ch 1, sc in same st and in next 5 sc, 2 sc in next sc, (sc in next 6 sc, 2 sc in next sc) around; join with slip st to first sc: 56 sc.

Rnd 9: Ch 1, sc in same st and in next 6 sc, 2 sc in next sc, (sc in next 7 sc, 2 sc in next sc) around; join with slip st to first sc: 63 sc.

Rnd 10: Ch 1, sc in same st and in next 7 sc, 2 sc in next sc, (sc in next 8 sc, 2 sc in next sc) around; join with slip st to first sc: 70 sc.

Rnds 11 and 12: Ch 1, sc in same st and in each sc around; join with slip st to first sc.

Rnd 13: Ch 1, sc in same st and in next 7 sc, sc2tog, (sc in next 8 sc, sc2tog) around; join with slip st to first sc: 63 sc.

Rnd 14: Ch 1, sc in same st and in next 6 sc, sc2tog, (sc in next 7 sc, sc2tog) around; join with slip st to first sc: 56 sc.

Rnd 15: Ch 1, sc in same st and in next 5 sc, sc2tog, (sc in next 6 sc, sc2tog) around; join with slip st to first sc: 49 sc.

Rnd 16: Ch 1, sc in same st and in next 4 sc, sc2tog, (sc in next 5 sc, sc2tog) around; join with slip st to first sc: 42 sc.

Rnd 17: Ch 1, sc in same st and in next 11 sc, sc2tog, (sc in next 12 sc, sc2tog) twice; join with slip st to first sc: 39 sc.

Rnds 18-20: Ch 1, sc in same st and in each sc around; join with slip st to first sc.

Do **not** finish off.

BRIM
Change to smaller size hook.

Row 1 (Wrong side)**:** Ch 1, turn; sc in first 16 sc, leave remaining 23 sc unworked: 16 sc.

Rows 2-4: Ch 1, turn; work beginning sc2tog, sc in next sc and each sc across: 13 sc.

Row 5: Ch 1, turn; sc in Front Loop Only of each sc across *(Fig. 2, page 44)*.

Rows 6-8: Ch 1, turn; working in both loops, 2 sc in first sc, sc in next sc and each sc across: 16 sc.

Finish off, leaving a long end for sewing.

Thread yarn needle with long end. Fold Brim in half to **wrong** side and sew sc on Row 8 to sc on Rnd 20 of Body.

Trim: With **right** side facing, using smaller size hook, and working in end of rows through **both** layers of Brim, join yarn with sc in first row *(see Joining With Sc, page 44)*; sc in next 2 rows, 3 sc in corner, sc in free loops of each sc across Row 4 *(Fig. 3a, page 44)*, 3 sc in corner; sc in next 3 rows; finish off.

STRAP
With smaller size hook, ch 23.

Row 1 (Right side)**:** Sc in second ch from hook and in each ch across: 22 sc.

Note: Mark Row 1 as **right** side.

Row 2 (Buttonhole row)**:** Ch 1, turn; sc in first sc, [ch 2, skip next 2 sc **(buttonhole made)**], sc in next 16 sc, [ch 2, skip next 2 sc **(buttonhole made)**], sc in last sc: 18 sc and 2 buttonholes (ch-2 sps).

Row 3: Ch 1, turn; sc in first sc, 2 sc in next ch-2 sp, sc in next sc and in each sc across to next ch-2 sp, 2 sc in next ch-2 sp, sc in last sc; finish off.

FINISHING
Using photo as a guide for placement, pin the Strap above the Brim; sew buttons to Body behind the buttonholes.

Button Strap to the Cap.

TEXTURED SET

 **EASY**

SHOPPING LIST

Yarn (Meduim Weight) 🄬4🄭
[3.5 ounces, 205 yards
(100 grams, 187 meters) per
skein]:
- ☐ **Hat** - One skein
- ☐ **Cowl** - One skein

Crochet Hook
- ☐ Size K (6.5 mm)
  or size needed for gauge

Additional Supplies
- ☐ 2¾" (7 cm) Buckle
- ☐ Yarn needle

SIZE INFORMATION

Hat: Fits head circumference
20-22" (51-56 cm)
Cowl: 8" wide x 21" circumference
(20.5 cm x 53.5 cm)

GAUGE INFORMATION

In pattern,
    12 sts and 10 rows/rnds = 4"
    (10 cm)
Gauge Swatch: 4" (10 cm) square
Ch 13.
Work same as Strap for 10 rows.
Finish off.

——— STITCH GUIDE ———

SINGLE CROCHET 2 TOGETHER
    (abbreviated sc2tog)
Pull up a loop in each of next 2 sts,
YO and draw through all 3 loops on
hook **(counts as one sc)**.

DOUBLE CROCHET 2 TOGETHER
    (abbreviated dc2tog)
    (uses next 2 sts)
★ YO, insert hook in **next** st, YO and
pull up a loop, YO and draw through
2 loops on hook; repeat from ★
once **more**, YO and draw through all
3 loops on hook **(counts as one dc)**.

INSTRUCTIONS
Hat
BODY

Ch 57 **loosely**; being careful **not** to twist ch, join with slip st to form a ring.

Rnd 1 (Right side)**:** Ch 2 (**counts as first hdc, now and throughout**), working in back ridge of beginning ch *(Fig. 1, page 44)*, (sc in next ch, dc in next ch) around; join with slip st to first hdc: 57 sts.

Note: Loop a short piece of yarn around any stitch to mark Rnd 1 as **right** side.

Rnd 2: Ch 2, turn; (sc in next dc, dc in next sc) around; join with slip st to first hdc.

Repeat Rnd 2 for pattern until Body measures approximately 5¾" (14.5 cm) from beginning ch, ending by working a **right** side rnd, do **not** finish off.

SHAPING

Rnd 1: Ch 2, turn; ★ (sc2tog, dc2tog) twice, (sc in next dc, dc in next sc) 3 times; repeat from ★ around; join with slip st to first hdc: 41 sts.

Rnd 2: Ch 2, turn; ★ sc2tog, dc2tog, (sc in next dc, dc in next sc) twice; repeat from ★ around; join with slip st to first hdc: 31 sts.

Rnd 3: Ch 2, turn; ★ sc2tog, dc2tog, sc in next dc, dc in next sc; repeat from ★ around; join with slip st to first hdc: 21 sts.

Rnd 4: Ch 2, turn; ★ (sc2tog, dc2tog) twice, sc in next dc, dc in next sc; repeat from ★ once **more**; join with slip st to first hdc: 13 sts.

Rnd 5: Ch 2, turn; (sc2tog, dc2tog) around; join with slip st to first hdc, finish off leaving a long end for sewing: 7 sts.

Thread yarn needle with long end and weave through sts on Rnd 5. Gather **tightly** and secure end.

STRAP

Ch 23.

Row 1 (Right side)**:** Working in back ridge of beginning ch, sc in third ch from hook **(2 skipped chs count as first hdc)**, dc in next ch, (sc in next ch, dc in next ch) across to last ch, hdc in last ch: 22 sts.

Note: Mark Row 1 as **right** side.

Rows 2-6: Ch 2, turn; (sc in next dc, dc in next sc) across to last hdc, hdc in last hdc.

Finish off, leaving a long end for sewing.

With **right** side facing, slip buckle onto Strap. Using photo as a guide for placement, sew Strap to Hat.

Cowl

Ch 63 **loosely**; being careful not to twist ch, join with slip st to form a ring.

Rnd 1 (Right side)**:** Ch 2, working in back ridge of beginning ch, (sc in next ch, dc in next ch) around; join with slip st to first hdc: 63 sts.

Note: Mark Rnd 1 as **right** side.

Rnd 2: Ch 2, turn; (sc in next dc, dc in next sc) around; join with slip st to first hdc.

Repeat Rnd 2 for pattern until Cowl measures approximately 8" (20.5 cm) from beginning ch, ending by working a **right** side rnd.

Finish off.

MODERN CHULLO

 **INTERMEDIATE**

Finished Size: Fits head circumference 20-22" (51-56 cm)

SHOPPING LIST

Yarn (Medium Weight)
[3 ounces, 145 yards
(85 grams, 133 meters) per skein]:
☐ Dk Grey - One skein
[3.5 ounces, 170 yards
(100 grams, 156 meters) per skein]:
☐ Red - One skein
☐ Grey - One skein

Crochet Hook
☐ Size J (6 mm)
   or size needed for gauge

Additional Supplies
☐ Yarn needle

GAUGE INFORMATON
14 sc = 4" (10 cm);
   5 rnds = 2¾" (7 cm)
Gauge Swatch: 2¾" (7 cm) diameter
Work same as Body for 5 rnds; do
not finish off.

——— STITCH GUIDE ———
SINGLE CROCHET 2 TOGETHER
   (abbreviated sc2tog)
Pull up a loop in each of first 2 sc,
YO and draw through all 3 loops on
hook (**counts as one sc**).

INSTRUCTIONS
BODY
With Dk Grey, ch 4; join with slip st
to form a ring.

Rnd 1 (Right side)**:** Ch 1, 7 sc in ring;
join with slip st to first sc.

Note: Loop a short piece of yarn
around any stitch to mark Rnd 1 as
right side.

Rnd 2: Ch 1, sc in same st and in
each sc around; join with slip st to
first sc.

Rnd 7: Ch 1, 2 sc in same st, sc in next 2 sc, (2 sc in next sc, sc in next 2 sc) around; join with slip st to first sc: 28 sc.

Rnd 8: Ch 1, sc in same st and in each sc around; join with slip st to first sc.

Rnd 9: Ch 1, 2 sc in same st, sc in next 3 sc, (2 sc in next sc, sc in next 3 sc) around; join with slip st to first sc: 35 sc.

Rnd 10: Ch 1, sc in same st and in each sc around; join with slip st to first sc.

Rnd 11: Ch 1, 2 sc in same st, sc in next 4 sc, (2 sc in next sc, sc in next 4 sc) around; join with slip st to first sc: 42 sc.

Rnd 12: Ch 1, sc in same st and in each sc around; join with slip st to first sc.

Rnd 13: Ch 1, 2 sc in same st, sc in next 5 sc, (2 sc in next sc, sc in next 5 sc) around; join with slip st to first sc: 49 sc.

Rnd 3: Ch 1, 2 sc in same st and in each sc around; join with slip st to first sc: 14 sc.

Rnd 4: Ch 1, sc in same st and in each sc around; join with slip st to first sc.

Rnd 5: Ch 1, 2 sc in same st, sc in next sc, (2 sc in next sc, sc in next sc) around; join with slip st to first sc: 21 sc.

Rnd 6: Ch 1, sc in same st and in each sc around; join with slip st to first sc.

Rnd 14: Ch 1, sc in same st and in each sc around; join with slip st to first sc.

Rnd 15: Ch 1, 2 sc in same st, sc in next 6 sc, (2 sc in next sc, sc in next 6 sc) around; join with slip st to first sc: 56 sc.

Rnd 16: Ch 1, sc in same st and in each sc around; join with slip st to first sc.

Rnd 17: Ch 1, 2 sc in same st, sc in next 7 sc, (2 sc in next sc, sc in next 7 sc) around; join with slip st to first sc: 63 sc.

Rnd 18: Ch 1, sc in same st and in each sc around; join with slip st to first sc.

Rnd 19: Ch 1, 2 sc in same st, sc in next 8 sc, (2 sc in next sc, sc in next 8 sc) around; join with slip st to first sc: 70 sc.

Rnd 20: Ch 1, sc in same st and in next 33 sc, 2 sc in next sc, sc in next 34 sc, 2 sc in last sc; join with slip st to first sc changing to Grey *(Fig. 4b, page 45)*; cut Dk Grey: 72 sc.

When changing colors while working Rnds 23-29, carry unused color on **wrong** side of work with normal tension; do **not** cut yarn unless otherwise specified.

Rnds 21-31: Ch 1, sc in same st and in each sc around following chart; join with slip st to first sc; at end of Rnd 29; cut Red and at end of Rnd 31, change to Dk Grey; cut Grey.

CHART

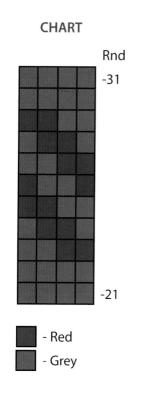

Rnd

-31

-21

■ - Red

▨ - Grey

Always follow chart from **right** to **left**.

Rnds 32 and 33: Ch 1, sc in same st and in each sc around; join with slip st to first sc.

Finish off.

FIRST EARFLAP

Row 1: With **right** side facing, skip first 11 sc and join Dk Grey with sc in next sc *(see Joining With Sc, page 44)*; sc in next 13 sc, leave remaining sc unworked: 14 sc.

Rows 2-11: Ch 1, turn; sc2tog, sc in next sc and in each sc across: 4 sc.

Row 12: Ch 1, turn; sc2tog, sc in next 2 sc: 3 sc.

Row 13: Ch 1, turn; sc2tog, sc in next sc: 2 sc.

Row 14: Ch 1, turn; sc2tog; finish off.

SECOND EARFLAP

Row 1: With **right** side facing, skip next 22 sc on Rnd 33 of Body from First Earflap and join Dk Grey with sc in next sc; sc in next 13 sc, leave remaining sc unworked: 14 sc.

Rows 2-11: Ch 1, turn; sc2tog, sc in next sc and in each sc across: 4 sc.

Row 12: Ch 1, turn; sc2tog, sc in next 2 sc: 3 sc.

Row 13: Ch 1, turn; sc2tog, sc in next sc: 2 sc.

Row 14: Ch 1, turn; sc2tog; finish off.

TRIM

With **right** side facing, join Grey with sc in first sc on Rnd 33 of Body; sc in next 10 sc, † sc in same sc on Rnd 33 as first sc on Row 1 of Earflap; working in ends of rows on Earflap, skip first row, sc in next 12 rows, skip last row, 3 sc in sc on Row 14; skip first row, sc in next 12 rows, skip last row; sc in same sc on Rnd 33 as last sc on Row 1 of Earflap †, sc in next 22 sc on Rnd 33, repeat from † to † once, sc in last 11 sc; join with slip st to first sc, finish off.

BRAID

Cut two 24" (61 cm) strands of each color yarn. Thread yarn needle with all 6 strands of yarn and pull yarn through center sc on one Earflap. With ends even, hold 4 strands of each color together. Work a 6½" (16.5 cm) braid; secure ends together with overhand knot, then trim ends.

Repeat for second Braid.

CUDDLY COWL

 EASY   *Shown on page 37.*

Finished Size: 27" (68.5 cm) circumference x 16" (40.5 cm) high

SHOPPING LIST

Yarn (Medium Weight)
[3.5 ounces, 170 yards
(100 grams, 156 meters) per skein]:
- ☐ Brown - 2 skeins
- ☐ Beige - One skein
- ☐ Black - One skein

Crochet Hook
- ☐ Size L (8 mm)
   or size needed for gauge

GAUGE INFORMATION

In pattern,
   8 sts and 8 rows/rnds = 3" (7.5 cm)
Gauge Swatch:
   3¾" (9.5 cm) square
Ch 11.
Row 1 (Right side)**:** Sc in second ch from hook and in next ch, ★ ch 2, skip next 2 chs, sc in next 2 chs; repeat from ★ once **more**: 6 sc and 2 ch-2 sps.
Rows 2-10: Ch 1, turn; sc in first 2 sc, ★ ch 2, skip next ch-2 sp, sc in next 2 sc; repeat from ★ once **more**. Finish off.

INSTRUCTIONS

With Brown, ch 72; being careful **not** to twist ch, join with slip st to form a ring.

Rnd 1 (Right side)**:** Ch 1, sc in same ch, ★ ch 2, skip next 2 chs, sc in next 2 chs; repeat from ★ around to last 3 chs, ch 2, skip next 2 chs, sc in last ch; join with slip st to first sc: 36 sc and 18 ch-2 sps.

Rnd 2: Ch 1, sc in same st, ★ ch 2, skip next ch-2 sp, sc in next 2 sc; repeat from ★ around to last ch-2 sp, ch 2, skip last ch-2 sp, sc in last sc; join with slip st to first sc.

Rnd 3: Repeat Rnd 2; at end of rnd, join with slip st to first sc changing to Beige *(Fig. 4b, page 45)*.

Do **not** cut Brown or Beige, carry unused yarns **loosely** along **wrong** side of work.

Repeat Rnd 2 working in the following Stripe Sequence:
★ one rnd Beige, one rnd Brown, one rnd Black, one rnd Brown, one rnd Beige, 3 rnds Brown; repeat from ★ 4 times **more**.

Finish off.

TOASTY SET

 **EASY**

SIZE INFORMATION
Hat: Fits head circumference
20-22" (51-56 cm)
Cowl: 6" wide x 72"
circumference (15 cm x 183 cm)

GAUGE INFORMATION
7 dc = 3¼" (8.25 cm);
3 rows/rnds = 2¼" (5.75 cm)
Gauge Swatch:
3¼" wide x 2¼" high
(8.25 cm x 5.75 cm)
Ch 9.
Row 1: Dc in fourth ch from hook
and in each ch across (**3 skipped
chs count as first dc**): 7 dc.
Rows 2 and 3: Ch 3 (**counts as first
dc**), turn; dc in next dc and in each
dc across.
Finish off.

—— STITCH GUIDE ——
**BEGINNING SINGLE CROCHET
2 TOGETHER**
  (abbreviated beginning sc2tog)
Pull up a loop in same sc as joining
and in next sc, YO and draw through
all 3 loops on hook (**counts as
one sc**).
SINGLE CROCHET 2 TOGETHER
  (abbreviated sc2tog)
Pull up a loop in each of next 2 sc,
YO and draw through all 3 loops on
hook (**counts as one sc**).

INSTRUCTIONS
Hat
BODY
Ch 3; join with slip st to form a ring.

Rnd 1 (Right side)**:** Ch 3 (**counts as first dc, now and throughout**), 11 dc in ring; join with slip st to first dc: 12 dc.

Note: Loop a short piece of yarn around any stitch to mark Rnd 1 as **right** side.

Rnd 2: Ch 3, dc in same st, 2 dc in next dc and in each dc around; join with slip st to first dc: 24 dc.

Rnd 3: Ch 3, 2 dc in next dc, (dc in next dc, 2 dc in next dc) around; join with slip st to first dc: 36 dc.

Rnd 4: Ch 3, dc in next 4 dc, 2 dc in next dc, (dc in next 5 dc, 2 dc in next dc) around; join with slip st to first dc: 42 dc.

Rnds 5-10: Ch 3, dc in next dc and in each dc around; join with slip st to first dc.

Rnd 11: Working from **left** to **right**, work reverse sc in each dc around *(Figs. 6a-d, page 46)*; join with slip st to first st, finish off.

TOPPER

Rnd 1 (Right side)**:** Ch 2, 6 sc in second ch from hook; join with slip st to first sc.

Note: Mark Rnd 1 as **right** side.

Rnd 2: Ch 1, 2 sc in same st and in each sc around; join with slip st to first sc: 12 sc.

Rnd 3: Ch 1, sc in same st, 2 sc in next sc, (sc in next sc, 2 sc in next sc) around; join with slip st to first sc: 18 sc.

Rnds 4 and 5: Ch 1, sc in same st and in each sc around; join with slip st to first sc.

Rnd 6: Ch 1, work beginning sc2tog, sc in next sc, (sc2tog, sc in next sc) around; join with slip st to first dc: 12 sc.

Rnd 7: Ch 1, work beginning sc2tog, sc2tog 5 times; join with slip st to first sc, finish off leaving a long end for sewing: 6 sc.

Stuff Topper with yarn.

Thread yarn needle with long end and sew Topper to top of Hat.

Cowl

Ch 155; being careful **not** to twist ch, join with slip st to form a ring.

Rnd 1 (Right side)**:** Ch 3, dc in next ch and in each ch around; join with slip st to first dc: 155 dc.

Rnds 2-8: Ch 3, dc in next dc and in each dc around; join with slip st to first dc.

Finish off.

GENERAL INSTRUCTIONS

ABBREVIATIONS

ch(s)	chain(s)
cm	centimeters
dc	double crochet(s)
dc2tog	double crochet 2 together
dtr	double treble crochet(s)
dtr2tog	double treble crochet 2 together
FPdtr	Front Post double treble crochet(s)
FPtr	Front Post treble crochet(s)
hdc	half double crochet(s)
hdc2tog	half double crochet 2 together
Ldc	Long double crochet(s)
mm	millimeters
Rnd(s)	Round(s)
sc	single crochet(s)
sc2tog	single crochet 2 together
sp(s)	space(s)
st(s)	stitch(es)
tr	treble crochet(s)
YO	yarn over

SYMBOLS & TERMS

★ — work instructions following ★ as many **more** times as indicated in addition to the first time.

† to † — work all instructions from first † to second † **as many** times as specified.

( ) or [ ] — work enclosed instructions **as many** times as specified by the number immediately following **or** work all enclosed instructions in the stitch or space indicated **or** contains explanatory remarks.

colon (:) — the number(s) given after a colon at the end of a row or round denote(s) the number of stitches or spaces you should have on that row or round.

CROCHET HOOKS															
U.S.	B-1	C-2	D-3	E-4	F-5	G-6	H-8	I-9	J-10	K-10½	L-11	M/N-13	N/P-15	P/Q	Q	S
Metric - mm	2.25	2.75	3.25	3.5	3.75	4	5	5.5	6	6.5	8	9	10	15	16	19

GAUGE

Exact gauge is **essential** for proper size. Before beginning your project, make the sample swatch given in the individual instructions in the yarn and hook specified. After completing the swatch, measure it, counting your stitches and rows or rounds carefully. If your swatch is larger or smaller than specified, **make another, changing hook size to get the correct gauge.** Keep trying until you find the size hook that will give you the specified gauge.

CROCHET TERMINOLOGY		
UNITED STATES		INTERNATIONAL
slip stitch (slip st)	=	single crochet (sc)
single crochet (sc)	=	double crochet (dc)
half double crochet (hdc)	=	half treble crochet (htr)
double crochet (dc)	=	treble crochet (tr)
treble crochet (tr)	=	double treble crochet (dtr)
double treble crochet (dtr)	=	triple treble crochet (ttr)
triple treble crochet (tr tr)	=	quadruple treble crochet (qtr)
skip	=	miss

■◻◻◻ **BEGINNER**	Projects for first-time crocheters using basic stitches. Minimal shaping.
■■◻◻ **EASY**	Projects using yarn with basic stitches, repetitive stitch patterns, simple color changes, and simple shaping and finishing.
■■■◻ **INTERMEDIATE**	Projects using a variety of techniques, such as basic lace patterns or color patterns, mid-level shaping and finishing.
■■■■ **EXPERIENCED**	Projects with intricate stitch patterns, techniques and dimension, such as non-repeating patterns, multi-color techniques, fine threads, small hooks, detailed shaping and refined finishing.

Yarn Weight Symbol & Names	LACE 0	SUPER FINE 1	FINE 2	LIGHT 3	MEDIUM 4	BULKY 5	SUPER BULKY 6
Type of Yarns in Category	Fingering, 10-count crochet thread	Sock, Fingering Baby	Sport, Baby	DK, Light Worsted	Worsted, Afghan, Aran	Chunky, Craft, Rug	Bulky, Roving
Crochet Gauge* Ranges in Single Crochet to 4" (10 cm)	32-42 double crochets**	21-32 sts	16-20 sts	12-17 sts	11-14 sts	8-11 sts	5-9 sts
Advised Hook Size Range	Steel*** 6,7,8 Regular hook B-1	B-1 to E-4	E-4 to 7	7 to I-9	I-9 to K-10.5	K-10.5 to M-13	M-13 and larger

*GUIDELINES ONLY: The chart above reflects the most commonly used gauges and hook sizes for specific yarn categories.

** Lace weight yarns are usually crocheted on larger-size hooks to create lacy openwork patterns. Accordingly, a gauge range is difficult to determine. Always follow the gauge stated in your pattern.

*** Steel crochet hooks are sized differently from regular hooks–the higher the number the smaller the hook, which is the reverse of regular hook sizing.

JOINING WITH SC

When instructed to join with sc, begin with a slip knot on hook. Insert hook in stitch or space indicated, YO and pull up a loop, YO and draw through both loops on hook.

BACK RIDGE

Work only in loops indicated by arrows *(Fig. 1)*.

Fig. 1

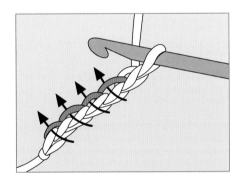

BACK OR FRONT LOOP ONLY

Work only in loop(s) indicated by arrow *(Fig. 2)*.

Fig. 2

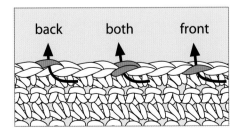

FREE LOOPS

After working in Back or Front Loops Only on a row or round, there will be a ridge of unused loops. These are called the free loops. Later, when instructed to work in free loops of same row or round, work in these loops *(Fig. 3a)*.

When instructed to work in free loops of a chain, work in loop indicated by arrow *(Fig. 3b)*.

Fig. 3a

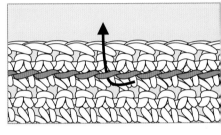

Fig. 3b

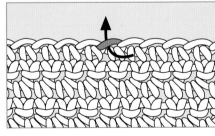

CHANGING COLORS

To change colors at the end of a row, work the last stitch to within one step of completion, drop yarn, hook new yarn *(Fig. 4a)* and draw through all loops on hook.

To change colors at the end of a round, drop yarn, with new yarn, join with slip st to first st *(Fig. 4b)*. Cut old yarn and work over both ends, unless otherwise instructed.

Fig. 4a

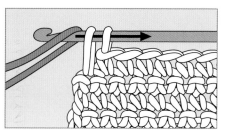

Fig. 4b

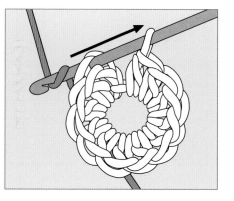

FRONT POST STITCH

Work around post of stitch indicated, inserting hook in direction of arrow *(Fig. 5)*.

Fig. 5

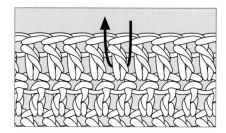

REVERSE SINGLE CROCHET

(abbreviated reverse sc)

Working from **left** to **right**, ★ insert hook in st to right of hook *(Fig. 6a)*, YO and draw through, under and to left of loop on hook (2 loops on hook) *(Fig. 6b)*, YO and draw through both loops on hook *(Fig. 6c)* (reverse sc made, *Fig. 6d*); repeat from ★ around.

Fig. 6a

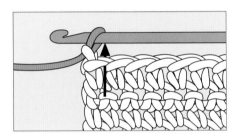

Fig. 6b

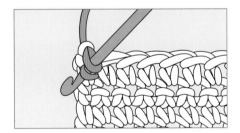

Fig. 6c

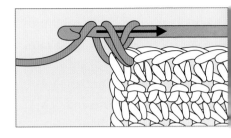

Fig. 6d

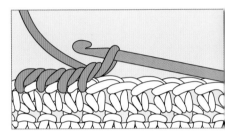

YARN INFORMATION

The projects in this book were made using various weights of yarn. Any brand of the specified weight of yarn may be used. It is best to refer to the yardage/meters when determining how many balls or skeins to purchase. Remember, to achieve the finished size, it is the GAUGE/TENSION that is important, not the brand of yarn.

For your convenience, listed below are the specific yarns used to create our photography models.

QUICK SCARF
Lion Brand® Wool-Ease®
Thick & Quick®
#138 Cranberry

SOFT RUFFLY SCARF
Lion Brand® Homespun®
#315 Tudor

MULTICOLORED SET
Lion Brand® Vanna's Choice®
Blue - #107 Sapphire
Lt Green - #170 Pea Green
Green - #174 Olive

CABLED SLOUCHY SET
Stitch Nation by Debbie Stroller®
Bamboo Ewe®
#5560 Grape

REVERSIBLE SCARF
Lion Brand® Vanna's Choice®
Blue - #109 Colonial Blue
Taupe - #099 Linen

BRIMMED CAP
Lion Brand® Vanna's Choice®
#400 Oatmeal

TEXTURED SET
Patons® Canandiana
#10744 Medium Teal

MODERN CHULLO
Lion Brand® Vanna's Choice®
Dk Grey - #404 Dark Grey Heather
Red - #113 Scarlet
Grey - #149 Silver Grey

CUDDLY COWL
Lion Brand® Vanna's Choice®
Brown - #126 Chocolate
Beige - #123 Beige
Black - #153 Black

TOASTY SET
Lion Brand® Homespun®
#366 Metropolis

Your

PLEASE SHARE
your comments and suggestions at
www.facebook.com/Official.LeisureArts

PLUS you can find us on Twitter,
Pinterest, and YouTube!!

opinion matters!

Production Team: Writer/Technical Editor - Sarah J. Green; Editorial Writer -
Susan Frantz Wiles; Senior Graphic Artist - Lora Puls; Graphic Artist - Jessica Bramlett;
Photo Stylist - Angela Alexander; and Photographer - Jason Masters.

Items made and instructions tested by Marianna Crowder and Raymelle Greening.

We have made every effort to ensure that these instructions are accurate and complete. We cannot,
however, be responsible for human error, typographical mistakes, or variations in individual work.